The **Essential** Bu

HILLM/

IMP

All models of the Hillman Imp, Sunbeam Stiletto,
Singer Chamois, Hillman Husky & Commer Imp
1963 to 1976

Your marque expert:
Tim Morgan

VELOCE PUBLISHING
THE PUBLISHER OF FINE AUTOMOTIVE BOOKS

www.veloce.co.uk

First published in May 2017 by Veloce Publishing Limited, Veloce House, Parkway Farm Business Park, Middle Farm Way, Poundbury, Dorchester, Dorset, DT1 3AR, England.
Fax 01305 250479/e-mail info@veloce.co.uk/web www.veloce.co.uk or www.velocebooks.com.

ISBN: 978-1-78711-009-0 UPC: 6-36847-01009-6

Introduction
– the purpose of this book

The Hillman Imp was born of the Rootes Group's desire to compete with BMC's Mini – and that was born of the need for a small, cheap-to-run car that was a step up from the proliferation of 'bubble cars' that had dominated the small car market. Whilst the Mini is always lauded (rightly) as a technical tour de force, the Imp wasn't exactly lagging behind. For space saving, it was fitted with a rear-mounted all-aluminium engine and transaxle that shared some DNA with the Coventry Climax racing engine. This lightweight powerplant pushed along a smart, genuine four-seater monocoque bodyshell, with ergonomic fingertip controls for the driver, and plush seating and interior trim.

The decision to build the car at the new Linwood factory, in Scotland, was a political and financial one – the Rootes Group wanted to manufacture the cars in its heartland in Coventry, but the government offered it grants and incentives to build an all-new factory in an area of mass unemployment, to try to kickstart the local economy. Much has been written about the issues, successes and failures of the new plant, but it is fair to say that the car gained a bad reputation for quality – some of it highly justified; some of this was due to the untrained workforce, some due to a rushed development program, and some down to penny pinching.

As was the fashion of the times, Rootes launched badge-engineered variants of the Imp, to try to appeal to as many potential buyers as possible. Using its

1976 Hillman Imp Basic – the last one ever made.

brand stables of Singer, Sunbeam and Commer, these variants covered luxury, performance and commercial vehicle markets. Some were more successful than others, but all have their own identities, and I shall cover all the different variants as part of this book.

440,000 Imps of various shapes, colours and creeds left the production line before the doors were closed in 1976. For many years, the Imp languished in the doldrums and was the butt of many automotive jokes. As a result, many were scrapped, and those that survived were often maintained on a shoestring – as buying a replacement car was sometimes cheaper than fixing one.

Today, enthusiasts are finally realising that the Imp can be a genuinely interesting, fun and viable alternative to BMC's offering. However, the path to finding a good example can be a tortuous one – as many examples have not been maintained to a high standard, and the Imp is one car that requires looking after. For many years, with values very low, Imps were often kept on the road by any means possible – with inevitable bodges, filler and poor quality repairs. With increased interest in the car, many examples offered for sale are simply tarted up, and not actually as good as they look. This book should help you to identify those cars and avoid buying trouble. A good Imp is a joyous car – let me help you find one.

Tim Morgan
Northamptonshire, England

Contents

The Essential Buyer's Guide™ currency
At the time of publication a BG unit of currency "●" equals approximately £1.00/US$1.26/Euro 1.18. Please adjust to suit current exchange rates using Sterling as the base currency.

1 Is it the right car for you?
– marriage guidance

Maintenance
An Imp needs maintenance – probably more so than any other car of its time. If the cooling system isn't maintained to peak performance, the car will overheat, leading to longer-term issues, such as warping the delicate alloy castings of the engine. You also need to use a torque wrench, and a good one at that – alloy is very easily stripped and distorted by excessive tightening; therefore the use of a torque wrench is essential. There aren't that many grease points – indeed the early cars didn't have any – and none of the maintenance is arduous, plus most jobs are fairly simple. Invest in a good workshop manual, as most jobs can be done at home by an enthusiast.

Parts supply
For a car that went out of production in the late 1970s, made by a company that hasn't existed for many years, the Imp is very well served for parts. However, bear in mind that you are unlikely to be able to pop down to Halfords to buy them! There are specialists who not only supply parts, but have also invested in remanufacturing many bespoke components to keep the cars on the road. There are many cross-over parts that were used on other British cars of the period – such as ignition components, some brake parts, etc. Additionally, the Imp Club can supply some spares, and there is plenty of advice available for finding alternatives.

Running costs
Generally speaking, Imps are very cheap to run. Fuel economy is superb – I have personally seen a genuine 55+mpg from my car on a long run – and consumable parts are inexpensive. Insurance is low, too, even for young drivers. The exception to this good news concerns panel prices. Replacement panels and repair sections can be expensive, especially if you're buying original equipment ones.

Club
The Imp Club is a fantastic resource for these cars. Not only does it help with keeping the cars on the road, there is a wealth of help, advice and support for anyone with an interest in the cars. It is also a wonderfully friendly club, with a good social side, and there are events organised all over the country (and in mainland Europe too) to meet up and enjoy the cars.

Using everyday?
Even on modern roads, the Imp is a highly capable car, and many owners still use their cars everyday. Obviously, the car will need a proper maintenance regime, but Imps tend to be more reliable when used in this fashion. If you are making the leap from a modern car to an Imp for everyday use, then you may need to consider such things as the drum brakes needing a little more effort (especially on non-servo equipped cars), and the heater system isn't as good as that of a modern car. There are also plenty of simple modifications that can be done to the car to assist with all-year round use.

Will it fit in the garage?

Unless you have a non-standard, tiny garage, the simple answer is yes. The standard Imp is 3.6m (141in) long by 1.5m (60in) wide and 1.4m (54.5in) tall – the van and Husky (estate) are approximately 10cm taller, and the coupé is roughly 2cm shorter.

Pros

Fun … driving an Imp is like driving a comfortable go-kart. The handling and roadholding are incredible, even in standard form. The interiors are nice places to be, with all cars having comfortable seating and a good driving position – even for tall drivers. The engines are like little turbines; these engines were designed to be high revving, and they thrive on being thrashed. The engine rarely sounds harsh and unpleasant, even at high engine speeds. The gear change should be near switch-like in its operation – with a slick synchromesh on all four gears. Visibility is amazing, you can see all four corners of the car from the driver's seat, making it a really easy car to drive.

Cons

Sadly, due to all those years when the cars were not worth much, many cars have suffered from neglect and bodging. As a result, some suffer from reliability issues – getting hot on motorways, clanking suspension, bad synchromesh, woolly steering and bad brakes are often indicators of neglect. Couple that with a tendency to leak water in the rain when the seals wear out: the cars can rust quite badly. Visible rust on Imps tends to be the tip of the iceberg, and restoration can be expensive, due to the complexity of the structure. A great many Imps have had less than stellar bodywork repairs done over the years, meaning that, whilst the paint may be shiny and smooth, what lies beneath may be poor.

Prices and investment potential

In recent years, the Imp and its derivatives have had a resurgence in interest. This has led to prices increasing dramatically. Some properly restored, rare models and genuinely good originals are changing hands for up to ●x10,000, and a good restoration project can cost around ●x1000. There are a lot of basket case cars that get roped into the 'restoration project' category that genuinely are not worth those sums – some are sadly worth more as parts than they are as cars.

In terms of investment, it is hard to say if values will continue to rise as they have. The survival rate is remarkably high, especially considering the low values of the past. However, finding a good, original car isn't so easy.

That leads me onto a very important point: there are very few original Imps left. The vast majority of Imps have been modified in some way or another, meaning that truly original cars can be very hard to find. As a result, you may pay a premium for a car in that condition. However, if you're planning to modify, it is often better to begin with an already modified one.

Alternatives

The obvious alternative is the Mini, although the prices of comparable period cars are often far greater than those of the Imp. Also consider the Austin 1100 range, the Fiat 126 (although the Imp is much more powerful), the Ford Anglia, or the Renault 8/10.

2 Cost considerations
– affordable, or a money pit?

Most Imp owners handle servicing and repairs on their own cars. Aside from the need for a torque wrench when working on the engine, most general servicing and repairs are fairly straightforward.

All the prices I've quoted are for parts, rather than the price a garage would charge you for the job.

Mechanical
Small service ●x50
Full service ●x120
Reconditioned engine (from) ●x800
Secondhand engine (from) ●x100
Reconditioned transaxle ●x500
Clutch kit ●x90
Brake shoes ●x30 (full car set)
Brake cylinders ●x15 each
Front dampers ●x120 pair
Rear dampers ●x80 pair
Trackrod ends ●x30 each
Road springs ●x90 car set

Gearboxes can be reconditioned by specialists.

Bodywork
The prices quoted are based on recent sales, but, in view of the scarcity of original panels, you may need to pay more.
Original front wings (new) ●x300 each
Original rear wings (new) ●x700 each
Original bonnet (new) ●x300
Original doors (saloon – new) ●x250 each
Wheelarches (aftermarket, from) ●x80 each
Floorpan (aftermarket) ●x75 per side
Outer sill (factory spec) ●x135 each
Lower rear corner (aftermarket) ●x70 each

Front wings, even secondhand ones, are hard to find.

Interior trim
With the exception of a few NOS rarities on eBay, there is no new factory interior trim left. Good secondhand seats, door cards, door cappings and dashboards occasionally come up for sale, but, as few cars are broken for spares these days (and those that are tend to be very poor examples), interior trim is very hard to find, and even harder to value.
Carpet sets (factory spec) ●x110

3 Living with a Hillman Imp
– will you get along together?

The Hillman Imp was designed, effectively, as the Rootes Group's version of the Mini concept. The Suez Crisis had meant that fuel costs had spiraled, and, as a result, initially, bubble cars had become very popular with the less well-off motorist. The Mini then showed that there was another way: small, lightweight cars that were frugal, and yet fun to drive, were being developed by many manufacturers, and the Rootes Group version was more than a little different.

With its low-slung, alloy engine mounted at the rear, ergonomic switch gear, and, on the early cars, an automatic choke, greaseless suspension and pneumatic throttle pedal, the Imp was technologically highly advanced. It was the brainchild of two young engineers, Tim Fry and Mike Parkes, and their youthful exuberance translated into a feisty little car. Its go-kart-like handling and revvy, race car-derived engine caused a few raised eyebrows at the distinctly conservative Rootes empire – indeed, the production cars were de-tuned, as the management believed that the prototypes were too fast.

However, problems with the car's rushed development meant that all was not rosy for the Imp – and, for many years, it has struggled to shake off a reputation for unreliability. Some of this, it has to be said, is justified, but it has to be looked at in context – in the early days, most mechanics were not used to working with unforgiving alloy engines, and so some of the problems stemmed from bad maintenance. Plus, there were some production difficulties. Later, when the cars were worth very little, many were poorly maintained, with similar consequences. Looked after properly, though, an Imp will be a joy to own.

An Imp is more than capable of everyday use, even on today's crowded roads. However, you must remember that the design is more than 60 years old, and some allowances have to be made. Unsurprisingly, many owners have modified their cars to cope better with the demands of the 21st Century: disc brakes, halogen headlamps, alternator conversions, and performance upgrades, are very common on Imps. In fact, it is fair to say that there are far more modified cars in existence than standard ones.

The Imp's cabin is a very pleasant place to be; light, airy, with extremely good all-round visibility (the Imp van less so, due to the lack of rear windows). The seats and trim are of high quality for their time, and you may be surprised how quiet a

Imps can more than keep up with modern traffic.

Sunbeam Imp Sports are very desirable for their improved performance.

standard Imp can be on the road. The noise and vibration are very well damped for such an old design, and an Imp can feel quite modern on the move.

The brakes on the standard cars are unservoed drums, and, as such, require a bit more pedal effort than a modern car, but have plenty of power. The steering is light and positive, with very light controls for the clutch. The gearbox is a joy – with synchros on all forward gears, changing up and down the box is a pleasure, not a chore. However, it is the engine that makes the car what it is.

Much has been written about the Imp's Climax-derived engine and its smooth, revvy nature. It wills you to hold onto gears for just a touch longer than you might in other cars, and it rewards you with progress that may surprise you. For such a small engine, it really can move, with only hills giving any clue to its diminutive size. It's quite a busy engine, though – 60mph is around 4000rpm, and this buzzy, revvy nature can be tiring on long motorway trips.

There is a surprising amount of space for luggage in the Imp – with room behind the back seat augmenting that under the front in the boot. There are a plethora of smaller spaces for loose items, such as the door bins, rear bins and even an area under the back seat. The Husky and van can carry astonishing amounts for their size – I have moved a washing machine in the back of a Husky with the seats down!

Spares are not too difficult to locate – there are a few specialists who stock all the essentials for keeping an Imp on the roads, and the costs of most items are reasonable. However, the days of popping to Halfords for service parts are long gone for this car.

The Imp Club is a wonderful resource too, with friendly advice, a great social scene and some parts supply.

As a result, living with an Imp in the 21st century is a highly attractive proposition, especially if you want to stand out from the crowd – it offers great smiles per gallon!

The social side of Imp ownership is encouraged by the Imp Club's events.

4 Relative values
– which model for you?

The Imp range is fairly complicated due to badge-engineering, and different iterations of the car.

In general, Imps are spoken of in terms of Mk1s ('63-'65), Mk2s ('65-'68) and Mk3s ('68-'76), even though the Mk3 designator was never officially used. The earlier cars (Mk1 and Mk2) are generally considered the more desirable and better built, but the Mk3 has many features that are improvements over the older cars.

A full listing of the models is shown in Chapter 17 – Vital statistics, so I've kept the descriptions brief and have expressed the values as a percentage of the the Sunbeam Imp Sport Mk2's value. Price guides in various classic car magazines will show you current values, but some models are worth more than others.

- Hillman Imp Mk1 (80%)
- Hillman Imp Mk2 – Super, DeLuxe or Basic (70%)
- Hillman Imp Mk3 – Super, DeLuxe or Basic (60%)
- Singer Chamois Mk1 (85%)
- Singer Chamois Mk2 (85%)
- Singer Chamois Mk3 (80%)
- Singer Chamois Sport (90%)
- Sunbeam Imp Sport Mk2 (100%)
- Sunbeam Imp Sport Mk3 (95%)
- Sunbeam Stiletto (100%)
- Hillman Husky (85%)
- Commer Imp Van (95%)

Late 1970s Hillman Imp Super.

Hillman Husky, post 1968 model.

Mildly modified Singer Chamois coupé.

5 Before you view
– be well informed

To avoid a wasted journey, and the disappointment of finding that the car does not match your expectations, it will help if you're very clear about what questions you want to ask before you pick up the telephone. Some of these points might appear basic, but when you're excited about the prospect of buying your dream classic, it's amazing how some of the most obvious things slip the mind ... Also check the current values of the model you are interested in in classic car magazines which give both a price guide and auction results.

Where is the car?
Is it going to be worth travelling to the next county/state, or even across a border? A locally advertised car may not sound very interesting, but can add to your knowledge for very little effort, so make a visit – it might even be in better condition than expected.

Dealer or private sale
Establish early on whether the car is being sold by its owner or by a trader. A private owner should have all the history, so don't be afraid to ask detailed questions. A dealer may have more limited knowledge of a car's history, but should have some documentation. A dealer may offer a warranty/guarantee (ask for a printed copy) and finance.

Cost of collection and delivery
A dealer may well be used to quoting for delivery by car transporter. A private owner may agree to meet you halfway, but only agree to this after you have seen the car at the vendor's address to validate the documents. Conversely, you could meet halfway and agree the sale but insist on meeting at the vendor's address for the handover.

View – when and where
It is always preferable to view at the vendor's home or business premises. In the case of a private sale, the car's documentation should tally with the vendor's name and address. Arrange to view only in daylight, and avoid a wet day. Most cars look better in poor light or when wet.

Reason for sale
Do make it one of the first questions: why is the car being sold, and how long has it been with the current owner? How many previous owners?

Left-hand drive to right-hand drive/specials and convertibles
If a steering conversion has been done, it can only reduce the value, and it may well be that other aspects of the car still reflect the specification for a foreign market.

Desirable models
Whilst the basic cars have their fans, it is fair to say that the Sunbeam and Singer models command a premium – often in excess of 25% over an otherwise standard car. Vans are very much in demand, and Husky models can be hard to find, therefore attracting a higher price.

Condition (body/chassis/interior/mechanicals)
Ask for an honest appraisal of the car's condition. Ask specifically about some of the check items described in Chapter 7.

All original specification
An original equipment car is invariably of higher value than a customised version – although such cars are very hard to find.

Matching data/legal ownership
Do VIN/chassis, engine numbers and licence plate match the official registration document? Is the owner's name and address recorded in the official document?

For those countries that require an annual test of roadworthiness (such as an MoT certificate in the UK), does the car have a document showing it complies? If a smog/emissions certificate is mandatory, does the car have one? If required, does the car carry a current road fund license/licence plate tag? Does the vendor own the car outright? Money might be owed to a finance company or bank: the car could even be stolen. Several organisations will supply the data on ownership, based on the car's licence plate number, for a fee. Such companies can often also tell you whether the car has been 'written-off' by an insurance company. In the UK these organisations can supply vehicle data:

DVSA	0300 123 9000	HPI	0845 300 8905
AA	0344 209 0754	DVLA	0844 306 9203
RAC	0800 015 6000		

Other countries will have similar organisations.

Unleaded fuel
If necessary, has the car been modified to run on unleaded fuel?

Insurance
Check with your existing insurer before setting out: your current policy might not cover you to drive the car if you do purchase it.

How you can pay
A cheque/check will take several days to clear and the seller may prefer to sell to a cash buyer. However, a banker's draft (a cheque issued by a bank) is as good as cash, but safer, so contact your own bank and become familiar with the formalities that are necessary to obtain one.

Buying at auction?
If the intention is to buy at auction, see Chapter 10 for further advice.

Professional vehicle check (mechanical examination)
There are often marque/model specialists who will undertake professional examination of a vehicle on your behalf. Owners' clubs will be able to put you in touch with such specialists.

Other organisations that will carry out a general professional check in the UK are:

AA	0800 056 8040	(motoring organisation with vehicle inspectors)
RAC	0330 159 0720	(motoring organisation with vehicle inspectors)

Other countries will have similar organisations.

6 Inspection equipment
– these items will really help

Before you rush out the door, gather together a few items that will help as you complete a more thorough inspection:

This book
Reading glasses (if you need them for close work)
Magnet (not powerful, a fridge magnet is ideal)
Torch (flashlight)
Probe (a small screwdriver works very well)
Overalls
Mirror on a stick/phone on selfie stick
Digital camera/phone camera
A friend, preferably a knowledgeable enthusiast

This book is designed to be your guide at every step, so take it along and use the check boxes to help you assess each area of the car you're interested in. Don't be afraid to let the seller see you using it.

Take your reading glasses if you need them to read documents and make close up inspections.

A magnet will help you check if the car is full of filler, or has fibreglass panels. Use the magnet to sample bodywork areas all around the car, but be careful not to damage the paintwork. Expect to find a little filler here and there, but not whole

panels. There's nothing wrong with fibreglass panels, but a purist might want the car to be as original as possible.

A torch with fresh batteries will be useful for peering into the wheelarches and under the car.

A small screwdriver can be used – with care – as a probe, particularly in the wheelarches and on the underside. With this you should be able to check an area of severe corrosion, but be careful – if it's really bad the screwdriver might go right through the metal!

Be prepared to get dirty. Take along a pair of overalls, if you have them. Fixing a mirror at an angle on the end of a stick may seem odd, but you'll probably need it to check the condition of the underside of the car. It will also help you to peer into some of the important crevices. You can also use it, together with the torch, along the underside of the sills and on the floor. A selfie stick and mobile phone can perform the same function.

If you have a digital camera, or your mobile phone has a good camera, take it along so that, later, you can study some areas of the car more closely. Take a picture of any part of the car that causes you concern, and seek a friend's opinion.

Ideally, have a friend or knowledgeable enthusiast accompany you: a second opinion is always valuable.

www.velocebooks.com / www.veloce.co.uk
Details of all current books • New book news • Special offers • Gift vouchers • Forum

15

7 Fifteen minute evaluation
– walk away or stay?

So you have driven to see your potential Imp purchase. Before you roll around on the floor looking underneath in detail at it, take a walk around the car slowly and look at all these key areas – if it checks out after this, then it is worth taking a more in-depth look. If not, you may be wasting your time.

Exterior

Begin by walking around the car, looking at how it sits. Does it sit level? Many standard Imps sit with their nose 'up' compared to the back. This isn't quite right, except on very early cars, and denotes that the rear springs may have sagged slightly over time – the fronts rarely wear – due to the lack of weight over them, but the reverse is true of the rears. New springs can be bought, but it is worth taking this into account.

Front wheelarch showing poor repairs and rust holes.

Now sight along the rear wings: Imps taper front to rear, and a surefire way of telling if the rear arches have been replaced properly is to look at the line of the rear wings. If the wings appear slab-sided in profile with no taper, then the car has had repair work done. In really poor cases, I have seen wheelarches tacked over the top of the rusty original arches and then filled, to lose the join. Feeling the inner lips of the arches will tell you a lot about how well any repairs have been done.

Whilst looking at the rear wings, look at the sill area. There should be a distinct step before the sill curves under the car – if not, it is likely that poor quality sill repairs have been carried out. Also look for a joint line between the main sill and the rear wing – on original cars and those that have had their sills replaced properly, this joint should be visible. If not, then it is highly likely that the car has cover sills; in that instance, it could take expensive repairs to put it right.

Cover sill fitted – whilst MoT-worthy, it may not be as strong as the original.

As you walk around the car, look for rust in the corners of the doors, front edge of the bonnet (and rear corners too), bottom corners of the engine lid, wheelarches and the lower part of the rear hatch (if a saloon). The hatch rusts along the section where the body seal is attached, and also where the two sections of the frame bolt together. New parts are impossible to find for this, and it's very hard to repair.

You may well find that the rear hatch stays are no longer working – there is a little roller peg that sits inside a nylon disc that operates the latching mechanism. Sadly, these nylon discs are affected badly by UV deterioration, and it is very common for them

Hatch supports suffer from UV damage, as seen here.

Husky rear doors rust from the inside out, and behind the rubber seal.

Rear corners of the bonnet rust, as does the front lip.

to no longer work. New ones are very hard to find, as are good secondhand ones.

If you are looking at a Husky, the condition of the tailgate is incredibly important, too – steel ones are impossible to find in good condition, although very good GRP ones can be bought for around ●x400. These tailgates rust on the outer panels along the bottom edge, but also check around the window aperture for signs of bubbling, repairs or filler – this is very common. Open the door and check the inner panel around the outer seal (there should be one fitted, but rarely is it in a good state). Also check the inner panel for signs of bubbling around the window aperture. Put simply, these tailgates rust pretty much everywhere.

Lift the bonnet, and check under the front for signs of accident damage – bent front chassis legs are quite common. Whilst this isn't necessarily the end of the world if the outer panels are straight, it can sometimes mean the shell is twisted. Likewise, it is well worth checking inside the engine bay for the same issue. Whilst looking in the lower corners of the engine compartment, check the state of the inner panels for signs of rust and/or repairs, as this is a common rot-spot.

Because Imps were previously not worth a great deal, they tended to be repaired on a tight budget; therefore it is very common to find filler and low quality welded repairs on the shell. In some cases, these repairs are hidden under very well applied recent paint, so it check thoroughly for tell-tale lumps and bumps that don't look 'right.'

Interior

Bearing in mind how few Imps are totally standard, the condition of the interior can vary greatly. Very few cars retain their standard steering wheels, as these are quite large. Very small steering wheels, conversely, will make the steering feel heavier than standard, and some Mountney-type centre hubs block vision of the temperature gauge. Feel the carpets in the front footwells, and lift the rubber mat in the rear – rain water leaks are very common on Imps, and can be the death of them. Screen seals are easily replaced and easily sourced, but if the interior is very damp, look very carefully at the floor, and establish the source of the dampness.

Are the seats the right ones for the car? What sort of condition are they in? Later Chrysler cars (post-1968) have seats with welded seams, making repairs

Highly modified Singer Chamois interior.

Headlinings split with age: Stiletto cloth (as shown) is hard to replicate.

much more difficult, so any tears may be tricky to repair invisibly. Early cars suffer from rotting stitching and seams coming undone – this isn't impossible to repair, but, unless you can do this yourself, it can be expensive.

Check the condition of the headlining, especially on Husky variants. Staining is easily removed, but tears mean it needs replacing. For Huskies, this is especially expensive, as it's a big job.

Engine

Is it the right specification engine for the car? See the reference guide for more details. Before starting it, look in the radiator for muck/oil – this may denote cooling system maladies, and even a potential head gasket failure. Look at the colour of the oil – if it is very black or smells 'burnt,' it indicates that the engine may have been neglected. Preferably,

An oily engine is a sign of neglect.

start the engine from cold, looking for oil smoke (or any other excessive smoke), and listen for rattles/knocks. Imp engines are nearly turbine smooth when in good order, so anything less means it could be a tired unit. It is worth mentioning that Imps were always supplied new with bright, clean bare aluminium-finished engines. Therefore if the car you are looking at is excessively black and dirty, it points to neglect and oil leaks that will need resolving.

If the car has been modified for higher performance, look at the quality of the work done to modify it. Also investigate in full parts that have been fitted to the car that did not begin life on an Imp – you need to be sure that you can source replacement parts, if anything fails in the future.

Cooling system

Possibly more than any other car, you must investigate the condition of the cooling system on any Imp you view. Look for signs of new parts, such as the water pump and the radiator. There is a rubber seal between the fan assembly and the radiator – this ensures that all the cooling air from the fan is pumped into the radiator: its condition is critically important. The good news is new ones are available.

The radiator needs to be cleaned regularly to ensure the gills do not get furred up with road film and grime. The only satisfactory way of doing this is to remove it from the car. Talk to the vendor about when this was last done.

Look at the colour of the coolant – an Imp needs a strong mix of good quality antifreeze to ensure that the delicate waterways do not get damaged. Again, this needs to be changed regularly, so ask the vendor when this was last done. Being an older engine, modern 'fit for life' coolants rarely work well.

Gearbox

Imps have a transaxle containing the gearbox and final drive assembly. It is a fairly inaccessible unit, meaning it is very often neglected, even by enthusiast owners. It should have synchromesh on all four forward gears, and should have a light, easy and positive change, despite the length of the linkage. The ball in the bottom of the lever wears with age and use, giving a floppy stick, plus the flexible linkage connecting the shaft to the transaxle wears, which makes obtaining reverse gear difficult.

Wheels and tyres

Most Imps rub the inner arches on full lock – so do not be alarmed if the one you are looking at does. From the factory, all Imps had steel wheels – 4J on the early cars (until around 1965), and 4.5J on all others. Depending on the spec of the car you are looking at, most should have small dome hub caps, with some models having an additional alloy embellisher ring. Sunbeam models always should have 'sunburst' full-size wheeltrims. These were also fitted to very late model 'Caledonian' limited edition cars.

Many Imps have aftermarket alloy wheels; make sure that they are the correct size; Imps have a 4x4in pcd stud pattern – centred on the studs, not the centre hub. Therefore, 100mm pcd wheels, whilst you may physically be able to fit them to the car, are not the right size and can potentially be lethal. If aftermarket wheels are fitted, check with the vendor as to their origin and sizes.

Badges and brightwork

Many Imps have been modified, so the exterior brightwork may not be quite as it left the factory. Compare what is fitted with the reference guide printed later in this book – although bear in mind that some things, such as over-riders on the bumpers were optional extras when the cars were new. New badges and external trim pieces are hard to find, so anything is damaged or missing could be tricky to put right.

Bumpers deserve a special mention, as they have a hard time and are easily damaged on Imps. The blades themselves are quite thick, but because they have long runs where they aren't supported, they pick up knocks and dents easily. The chrome itself was of very high quality when it was new, but many Imps now have quite pitted chrome due to the effects of age. Very few bumpers can be found new, especially the standard Imp rear bumper – occasionally you will see Imp Sport rear bumpers with the holes in them for the numberplate lamps. Rechroming is an option for a car with bad bumpers, but bear in mind that straightening them can be very tricky, if they have been bashed as well.

Paperwork

Only buy a Hillman Imp from an individual who can prove that they are the person named in the car's registration document (V5C in the UK) and, preferably, at the address shown in the document. Also check that the VIN or chassis number and engine numbers of the car match the numbers in the registration document.

Make sure that the log book for the car corresponds with what you are looking at. As with many classic cars, Imps can sometimes be the target for the unscrupulous – look out for late model cars where the identity has been changed to an earlier one, to save paying road tax, etc. The reference guide at the end of the book can be very useful for determining this, and, if in any doubt, get a second opinion from an expert.

You will find the chassis plate either on the left-hand side of the engine bay in very early cars or on the front slam panel on later cars. Be wary of fresh-looking pop-rivets securing this – except in the case of some late model cars which have the chassis number stamped into the inner wing panel, this is the only place that a shell is marked with the number.

Modifications

As I have mentioned already, Imps are rarely found in factory specification.

Historically, they have always been modified – indeed, books were written in the 1960s on how to modify the Imp. Therefore, if you are after an original car, you may well be holding out for a long time. If you are not worried, or indeed you want a car that is slightly (or more than slightly) modified, only you can decide whether those modifications enhance, or otherwise, the car you are looking at.

I would urge caution with a car that has lots of 'extras' fitted – look carefully at the quality of installation. For example, Imp wiring looms (with the exception of very late model ones) do not have fuse boxes from the factory and therefore lots of electrical extras can put quite a strain on an already old wiring loom.

However, some modifications can be an improvement. Early Mk1s were positive earth from the factory and many have been converted to negative, to allow the fitment of these extras – but, due to a quirk in the loom, there really needs to be a relay installed to operate the horn for cars that have been converted. Without this, such cars can suffer nasty wiring fires, in certain circumstances.

Performance modifications are the most common – usually uprating a standard car to Imp Sport or beyond. Again, look carefully at the quality of the workmanship that has been done and ask the vendor about anything you aren't sure of.

Walk away or stay?

Imps are hard to find and it is very easy to get carried away with a car purchase. You need to be pragmatic, though – if you have looked thoroughly at all the areas detailed above and still are interested, it is worth turning to Chapter 9 – Serious evaluation to take your investigation further.

However, if you have uncovered a lot more work than you were prepared to do, I would suggest walking away at this point. Experience tells me that, often, with any classic car, if you find something you aren't happy with, especially corrosion, it can be the tip of an expensive iceberg. If the car is cheap, bear in mind that the costs of repairing it to your satisfaction will often exceed the difference between a cheap car and another, that looks more expensive, but is ultimately in better condition.

Buying any classic car should never be an emotive decision, but usually is. Be objective at this point, and you can save yourself a lot of expense and heartache later. But that is easier said than done!

Plenty of Imps are modified by their owners.

8 Key points
– where to look for problems

Pay particular attention to the following areas:

Sills
Check the outer sills. Have they been changed? If they have, are the outer panels the correct specification? Move the carpet on the inside, and try to feel the inner sill structure between the floor and box section that carries the heater pipes – there should be a vertical solid steel panel: if this is crunchy or missing, the structure of the car will be massively weakened.

Sill structure critical – this one will need replacing and it's not a small job.

Floor edges
The edges of the floor corrode, especially at the rear corners, just in front of the rear wheelarches. Look out for patches, and make sure any repairs have been done

properly. Look out for repair patches that have been welded to the floor and the bolt-in rear crossmember (common bodge).

Check the condition of the floorpan, especially at the rear.

Wheelarches
Imp arches are double skinned, and moisture gets trapped between the panels, rotting out both the inner and outer panels. Some previous repair work can be questionable, so look closely.

Wheelarches rust from the inside out.

Interior trim

Look out for torn seats, cracked dash tops, and water damage. Next to no new trim is available, and secondhand parts are getting harder to source. Professional retrimming is an option but getting the correct materials/finish can be tricky and expensive.

Original interiors, such as this Chamois one, are hard to find.

Engine/mechanical

Look for a neglected cooling system causing overheating. Neglect and high mileage can cause smoke, rattles and excessive oil leaks.

Check the cooling system carefully: look for leaks, also sludge in the coolant.

9 Serious evaluation
– 60 minutes for years of enjoyment

Circle Excellent (4), Good (3), Average (2) or Poor (1) for each check, and add up points at the end. Any evaluation check must be realistic. Sole responsibility lies with the buyer to be vigilant and not cut corners over the next 60 minutes. Take it seriously, get it right, and you will be able to make an informed decision on whether to purchase. Get it wrong, and it could become your worst nightmare.

The main shell of the Imp didn't change in its construction throughout its lifetime. So the same places to check apply to all variants of the Imp, with a few extra ones for the coupé and van/Husky shells.

Outer sills

You can't spend too much time checking the sill and floor edges. The sill is a complex structure, with a main outer section that begins *behind* the front wing corner, passes under the door and then passes behind the rear wing to attach to the inner structure under the back seat. There are closing sections that are part of the front and rear wing that cover the extremes of the sill – these double-skinned areas rust due to condensation. If the sills have been replaced, view the car very carefully, and quiz the owner on how it had been done, by whom and with what panels. A lot of cars were fitted with skin sills, or cover sills, years ago, that add nothing to the rigidity of the shell – and, unless you are looking to replace them long-term, should be avoided.

Outer sills need thorough checking – with gentle finger pressure, this bubble soon became a hole.

Inside box section

Inside the car, there is a box section that contains the front-to-back heater pipes and, on the driver's side, the wiring loom. The bottom edge of this can corrode unseen, on cars that have been stored in damp conditions or where a lot of condensation can occur.

Inner membrane sill

Between the box section and the outer sill lies a membrane inner sill; this ties the sills to the floor. This is critical in maintaining the incredible strength of the Imp shell – without it, or if it is breached, the sill no longer acts as part of the box and no longer keeps the cornering forces from acting on the shell. In short, the shell becomes very flexible, and, in extreme cases, the car no longer drives properly.

To check the condition of the inner membrane, lift the carpet from the inner box along its bottom and attempt to slide your fingers between the floorpan and the box. Be VERY careful not to slice your finger open doing this on rusty metal. You should feel a strong, smooth steel upright section at the back of it. Whilst you are in there, try squeezing the box section – it should not move at all. Any crunching noises could be expensive. Try this along the whole length of the sill, where practical.

In the bottom of the rear luggage bins, there is a hardboard cover (usually vinyl covered). If you remove this and shine your torch inside, you can see the rear section of the sill, plus the heater hose (this will give you an idea of the condition of these).

On a car where the inner sill is breached, crunchy, or in any way dodgy, the only way to fix it involves the removal of whatever outer sills are fitted.

Properly replacing the sills on an Imp is a very labour-intensive job, and

Slide your fingers under the inner box section to check inner membrane sill.

quality sill panels are not cheap: replacement of the sills could end up costing a four-figure sum.

Rear box sections

Whilst you are in this area of the car, lift the rear seat. Under the seat squab (and any soundproofing fitted), you will find some small box sections. With the aid of your torch and your fingers carefully examine their condition. This is the area that the rear crossmember bolts to, and, again, it's critical to find this in good order. Above the seat pan, there are two chassis legs that are spot welded to the shell – inspect the areas around these carefully, and be suspicious of any repair work. Also, look for signs of damp ingress: the rear hatch (and rear screen on the coupé) is renowned for letting in water, and it can collect in the box sections under the rear seat, with inevitable results.

Check box section under the rear seat carefully,

Floorpans

Check the floorpan very carefully. Where the floor meets the sill is a favourite rot-spot, and often repairs in this area are not carried out very well. Any patches here should be viewed with caution – was the rot cut out or was it just an MoT patch? A proper repair involves a lot of cutting and welding – until recently replacement floorpans were not available and therefore some cars resemble patchwork quilts underneath.

Check carefully the condition of the floor in the rear corners, around the bolt-in crossmember. This is an area where patches can often be found. Rainwater can leak into the car through the rear hatch and collects in the box sections mentioned earlier. This area is critical to the rear strength of the shell and must be repaired properly, which involves removing the bolt-in rear crossmember

Front corners of the floor can rot due to leaky windscreen seals.

that sits under the rear floor. This is rarely done, due to the labour-intensive nature of the job. It is not uncommon to find cars where patches have been applied to the rear floorpan and welded to the rear bolt-in crossmember, rather than removing it properly. This takes a lot of unpicking, so avoid cars than have been badly repaired here.

Rainwater leaks can cause holing around the edge of the floor where it joins the inner front wheelarches. Investigate any sign of corrosion there – if it is just surface rust, it can sometimes be saved with cleaning and treating, but often the panels get so thin it is only sensible to cut it out and replace the steel.

Inside the car, it is worth checking around the front seat mounting points. This area of the floor often tears around the bolt holes, leading to insecure seats.

Rear suspension cones

Examine the inner rear wheelarches; behind the wheels there should be cone-shaped panel where the road spring locates. This panel, and the surrounding steel, corrode behind any underseal applied. If there appears to be a large amount of underseal here, check carefully – plating and patches are very common here. Repairing this area properly isn't easy, and its rare to find an Imp where this has been done to factory standards. Inside the car, this is hidden by the rear seat and the vinyl cover over the inner

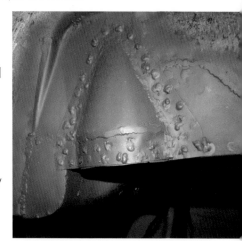

Rear suspension cone – lots of work is required to repair one to this standard.

arch: it is worth having a prod around this area from inside the car, too, but be careful not to tear the vinyl on the inner wheelarch, as it is normally very well stuck.

Inner rear arches   4️⃣ 3️⃣ 2️⃣ 1️⃣

The rear inner wheelarches often rot at the end of the sills too – patches here aren't too critical, but try to work out whether it's a plate over the rust, or if the corrosion was cut out before the patch was applied. The lower rear corner of the wing is another place to check for filler/rust – your low-strength fridge magnet will reveal its true condition, if you have any doubts over it.

Lower rear corners and inner wheelarches rust through.

Check the inner and outer sections of the wheelarch, and where the tub meets the sill.

Outer wheelarches   4️⃣ 3️⃣ 2️⃣ 1️⃣

I touched on the condition of the wheelarches in the 15 minute evaluation, but it bears repeating that the condition of the arches is important. Run your hand around the inside of the rear arches: you are looking for lumps of filler, glass fibre, or, worse still, holes. View any cars with large amounts of fresh underseal, here, with caution.

Rear light area   4️⃣ 3️⃣ 2️⃣ 1️⃣

Look carefully around the rear lights; this is a double-skinned area, and the tin worm finds it particularly tasty. It is very common to find bubbles and filler here – so check carefully, as it's not easy to repair, and repair sections for this area are not easy to come by.

Repairs to the light area can be tricky.

Doors

Moving forwards, feel the bottom of the doors for filler. Imp doors rot in the bottom corners, from the inside out – usually as a result of bad door seals, but also from condensation in the extreme corners.

While you're checking the doors, look for cracks in the frame where the frame meets the top of the door skin. Also look for 'bagging' under the quarterlight – there is a small strap panel that holds the inner frame to the skin, just under the quaterlight and this can break/tear, especially with heavy-handed slamming, etc. In extreme cases, the rubber seal around the quaterlight fails, leading to water ingress into the door and, hence, into the car.

Bottom corners of the doors warrant inspection.

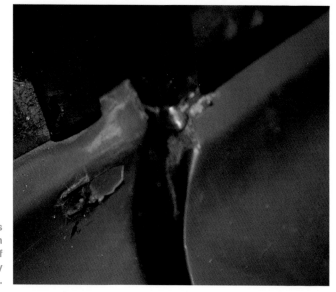

Door frames can split from the doors, if continually slammed.

28

Rear hatch

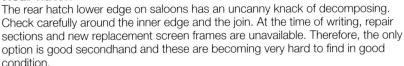

The rear hatch lower edge on saloons has an uncanny knack of decomposing. Check carefully around the inner edge and the join. At the time of writing, repair sections and new replacement screen frames are unavailable. Therefore, the only option is good secondhand and these are becoming very hard to find in good condition.

Rear hatch lower section rusts behind the seal. Check carefully.

Rear hatch aperture

The steel under the seal can rust away unseen. Factory paint was never very thick at this point, and the seal traps moisture very effectively under it. On late model cars, there are drain channels in the bottom corners of this aperture which are very effective (and worth replicating if this area needs replacing), but they don't prevent rusting of this area.

Check the rear hatch aperture for rusting under the seal

Rear edge of the roof

Until around 1973, Imp saloons had three vents under the lip of the roof. This was to provide airflow through the cabin of the car. However, this was deleted on later cars – it

Three vents across the back of the roof on cars pre-1973.

is said that this was due to fume ingress on cars fitted with them that had less-than-perfect engine compartment sealing. As a result, the box section at the back of the roof can attract moisture and condensation leading to rusting of the roof skin. This isn't an easy repair, so be wary of any bubbling here.

Van/Husky rear door 4️⃣ 3️⃣ 2️⃣ 1️⃣

On Huskies and vans, the rear door condition is pretty important. The outer skin rots pretty much everywhere, but look especially around the window and along the bottom edge. Filler is very common here, as proper repairs are hard to achieve. Also, look carefully around the window inside the door, and along the bottom edge. New steel doors are nearly impossible to find, with good secondhand ones almost as difficult to locate. You can buy replacement doors in GRP that are superb quality and are weighted so they become almost indistinguishable from steel. Frankly, these are viewed as an upgrade by most owners, but they are not cheap.

Van/Husky rear doors suffer badly from internal corrosion. Few are this good.

Coupé rear screen box section 4️⃣ 3️⃣ 2️⃣ 1️⃣

On coupé models, check the box section under the rear screen very carefully. You may need to remove the rubber mat (or roll it out of the way); the steel is covered by a hardboard panel, covered in vinyl. This is clipped to the steel beneath by small (easily broken!) clips. If you can remove the inner trim to access it, then it is worth

Rust affects the box section under the rear window of coupé shells.

checking – ask the vendor first, before doing so. It is also worth lifting the engine lid a little to check the condition of the channel behind the lid – this is the back of this box section.

Door hinge mountings

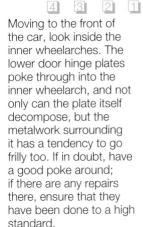

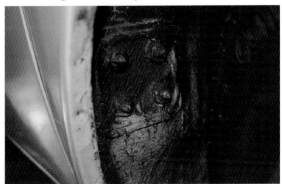

The door hinge plate in front inner wheelarch rusts, as does surrounding metalwork.

Moving to the front of the car, look inside the inner wheelarches. The lower door hinge plates poke through into the inner wheelarch, and not only can the plate itself decompose, but the metalwork surrounding it has a tendency to go frilly too. If in doubt, have a good poke around; if there are any repairs there, ensure that they have been done to a high standard.

H-brackets

The front damper/spring mounts are sited within an H-bracket inside the inner wing tubs. These are open to the elements, and, as such, get all manner of mud and detritus thrown up onto the flat top section. If unchecked and cleaned, this mud will cause the inner wing tub to breach. It is also worth checking the condition of the whole H-bracket, as they are very vulnerable. You may need to jack the front of the car up and remove the road wheel to view this area properly – either way, you will need a torch. Feel the very top of the H-bracket, where the damper bolts in – this nut should be tight against the top of the retainer. Any gap here can mean that the centre of the spring retainer has split – this is a bolt-in panel.

Lift the bonnet and remove the inner cardboard inner-wing covers – they are held in by some steel tabs that need to be carefully bent out of the way. The tank may be in the way of a thorough inspection, but a mirror on a stick could be useful here. If positioned correctly, you should be able to see two bolt heads going into the inner wing. Above this, but below the top of the tank, is where this panel rots. Look

Inner wing rusted behind H-bracket – tank removed for clarity.

carefully here for signs of rust or repairs. Very often these repairs consist of a piece of bent steel tacked over the top of the corrosion – if that is the case, this will need to be repaired properly which involves stripping down most of the front end of the car.

Some cars will have been modified by 'turreting' the top of the H-bracket. This involves welding a plate over the top of the H-bracket in the wheelarch; then cutting the inner wheelarch panel away on the inside of the car to provide access to the spring mountings. This is a massive improvement over the original design, but it needs to have been done to a high standard.

Front wheelarches

As with the rear arches, these are double-skinned panels, and both the inner and outer skins suffer. The outer panels are often repaired with filler on poor examples, especially at the bottom where the arch covers the end of the sill.

Run your hand around the inside of the lip, feeling for fibreglass, filler and holes.

The vertical section of the tub just under the door hinge mounts can rot through, leading to a 'mouse hole' in the end of the sill. If that has happened, the sill is likely to be in a poor state inside, as it will be filling up with water in rainy conditions. Have a very good feel around here for crunchy areas and previous repairs.

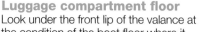

Front outer wheelarches are often poorly repaired with filler.

Luggage compartment floor

Look under the front lip of the valance at the condition of the boot floor where it joins the outer panels. Also, look carefully for cracks or corrosion around the two large bolts that attach the front wishbones to the floor. View any repairs with caution, but you may be able to look from above to see if any corrosion has been cut out. If the car has been modified with a front-mounted radiator, check carefully for evidence of added stiffening in this area; the air intake plenum chamber on the front panel of the Imp has to be removed to fit a front-mounted radiator: as it provides a lot of stiffening for that part of the car, without it, there should be some degree of bracing

Lower front panel and inner boot floor can rust through – investigate any bubbles.

to the floor and the front panel to retain the strength.

Rear shelf [4] [3] [2] [1]

On cars where the rear screen has been leaking badly, the horsehair soundproofing will have trapped water against the rear shelf. This has a bitumastic coating that cracks over time, leading to water tracking under the bitumen in the gullies of the shelf. It is worth lifting this mat and looking for signs of corrosion to the shelf – in extreme cases, this shelf can hole badly.

Rear shelf suffers when the rear hatch leaks: an early car shown with extra stiffening.

Bonnet [4] [3] [2] [1]

The front edge of the bonnet often rots through – check both the inner frame and the outer skin thoroughly. It is also worth checking the rear corners for filler and/or rust. New steel bonnets are very hard to find, and secondhand replacements in good order are a rarity, but there are some excellent quality GRP ones available that offer a sensible alternative.

Front lip of the bonnet rusts from behind – also check the inner structure.

Bulkhead edges [4] [3] [2] [1]

It is worth checking the corners of the front bulkhead for holes, or evidence of repairs. This is an awkward area to repair properly: holes here can cause rain-water leaks and corrosion elsewhere, so it needs to be sound.

Ends of the scuttle rust from the inside, and are not easy to repair properly.

Coupé screen pillars

4 3 2 1

On coupé models, especially Stilettos, check the condition of the windscreen and the rear screen pillars – front and rear. On Stilettos, this area is covered by vinyl which can trap moisture behind it, rotting the steel unseen. Press firmly with your thumb and listen carefully for crunchy noises. It is worth running your hand over the edges of the entire vinyl roof, feeling for lumps and bumps, indicating that the steel underneath is corroding. In extreme cases, I have seen otherwise-good cars have holes appear under the vinyl, where the steel has rusted right though unseen.

Lumps under the vinyl roof on a Stiletto denote unseen corrosion.

Van/Husky roof seam and gutters

4 3 2 1

One of the big problem areas on the Husky/van shell is the roof panel, where it meets the gutters. This is a notorious rot-spot, and is not easy to repair successfully – and certainly not without stripping out the headlining, which can rend it ruined. Any obvious rust or repair work may well be the tip of the iceberg; it is expensive to fix, and not an easy DIY job.

Van/Husky gutters and roof edges are common rot spots.

Rubbers

[4] [3] [2] [1]

One of the big killers of Imp shells is water leaks; look at the condition of all the window rubbers. Whilst the main seals are easy to find for saloons, for the coupé and van/Husky it can be hard to find good quality replacement seals for some of the windows. The rubber seals beneath the wiper spindles can be problematic for leaking, too.

Exterior trim

[4] [3] [2] [1]

Check that the trim fitted to the car you are viewing is correct for its specification and year. Any damaged or missing pieces of the stainless steel wing trims will be hard to source – there is very little available new, and not a lot of it survives in good condition secondhand for some models. Rootes-era badges do not tend to survive well, as the paint is liable to delaminate from the clear plastic – this is easily repainted, but sometimes the plastic itself cracks. In some cases, the plastic centre can fall out of the badge surround, and can be hard to find.

Early type badging is hard to track down for rarer variants.

Interior trim

[4] [3] [2] [1]

Early cars had traditional seats with stitched vinyl covers and are generally very hard wearing. However, the stitching can rot, as can the foam itself. Check for split seams, and look under the seats for evidence of the foam falling to bits.

Later cars had welded seam seats, and generally do not wear as well. The diaphragms in the front seat squabs can fail, leading to ripping of the vinyl from the weight of the occupant. Repairs in this case can be tricky.

The dashboard top, especially in Stilettos and later cars, can split. Undamaged dash tops are hard to locate. Recovering is an option, but it rarely looks exactly the same as the original finish.

The headlining material in the early cars gets very brittle with age, leading to splits. This exact type of material is no longer obtainable, but headlining kits are available in different materials. The headlining in a Husky is particularly vulnerable

Early type seats can split along the seams.

Later seats had a welded pattern, and are not so easy to repair.

Early type headlings are quite fragile and tear easily.

Top of Mk3 dashboards split due to UV damage.

and also particularly expensive to replace. The headlining in a coupé is actually glued directly to the metal and is much easier to replace.

Water leaks can render the door cards warped and baggy. There should be a plastic liner inside the door to direct any water away from the hardboard-backed door cards, which is usually missing. For cars that have vinyl-covered cards, the vinyl can be carefully removed and re-applied to new cards made from hardboard. For base model cars with millboard cards, remanufacture is the only option.

Door cards warp due to water ingress from behind.

Electrics

There isn't a huge amount of electronic equipment in a Hillman Imp. However, the loom passes through the sill and around the rear wheelarch on the driver's side – so if any repairs have been done to the bodywork, moving the loom out of the way before any welding is done is critical. Carefully inspect the loom for any alterations and additions. Apart from the very late (post 1975) cars, Imps do not have fuse boxes, therefore the integrity of the loom is very important. Ensure any alterations have been done to a high standard, including changing from dynamo to alternator – many Imps have had this conversion.

4 3 2 1

Check that any modifications to the wiring have been done properly.

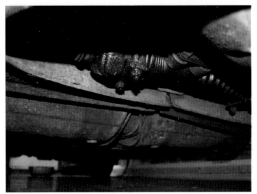

Leaking steering rack gaiter is an MoT fail and will cause wear.

Steering [4] [3] [2] [1]

Imp steering is by a rack and pinion system with kingpins providing the swivel for the front wheels. Jack the car up, and rock the wheel up and down to test for wear in the kingpins, and from side to side to test for wear in the trackrod ends. Parts are easy to locate, and, aside from freeing off seized fixings and getting stubborn king pins out, neither are difficult jobs. Look for leaks, and splits from the steering rack gaiter, whilst you have the car in the air.

Gearbox [4] [3] [2] [1]

The gearbox and final drive of an Imp should be a delight to use, with no graunching or whines. The synchros wear with age, so test thoroughly at normal road speeds – you shouldn't need to double de-clutch going up or down the box. The stick should feel like a switch – any free play denotes wear in the linkage, or the ball at the bottom of the stick itself. Look underneath for oil leaks from the output spiders, and ask the vendor when they last changed or checked the gearbox oil.

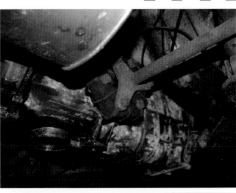

Check gearbox for signs of oil leakage.

Rotoflexes [4] [3] [2] [1]

Imps use rubber Rotoflex joints to connect the driveshafts to the gearbox. There are varying grades of quality for these, but the general rule of thumb is to inspect the joints for cracking – any sign of cracking means that they will need replacing soon. If they break, the flailing driveshaft can cause a lot of damage, even if only pulling away.

Rubber Rotoflex driveshaft couplings suffer from cracking.

Immaculate Imp Sport engine bay.

Engine

The engine won't tolerate neglect and/or abuse for long, so look for signs of both –
dirty oil, oil leaks, etc. Before starting the engine, look in the radiator – the fluid level
should be to the level of the plate that is just below the filler neck/expansion area.
Dip your finger into the coolant – if it feels oily, it could be a sign of head gasket
failure. Ask the vendor to start the car whilst you watch the coolant – bubbles
coming through the coolant are a sign that the head gasket isn't sealing properly,
especially if the bubbles increase with revving.

Look for oil smoke on start-up – blue smoke – and let the engine tick over for
a few moments and then blip the throttle again, looking for blue smoke again. A
reasonable amount of steam is normal due to the shortness of the exhaust, but any
blue smoke denotes either worn valve guides or piston rings.

Listen to the engine; it should be smooth, and should not be rattly. Setting the
valve clearances is achieved by using shims; due to the fiddly nature of this task, it is
rarely done, but can dramatically affect the performance of the engine.

Check the condition of the pipework in the engine bay; Imp cooling systems
are marginal when working *well*, so any potential for leaks should be avoided at all
costs. Look for evidence of weeping joints, as this can lead to air locks, causing
overheating or a lack of heater.

Imp waterpumps can be damaged by
overtightened fan belts.

The water pump front bearing is
an overstressed part, and the tension
of the fan belt is critical to keeping it
working well. The belt should not be
super tight – no less than an inch of
deflection along the longest run should
be felt. Overtightened belts can damage
the bearings. Also look at the colour of
the coolant – it should be maintained
with a good anti-freeze mix, otherwise
the internal waterways of the engine can
be damaged. In an ideal world, distilled
water should be used with the antifreeze,
to ensure that there isn't a build up of
mineral deposits inside the engine and
radiator.

Modified Imps often have uprated engines – carefully check the quality of the work.

The radiator needs to be in tip-top condition, and cleaned inside and out on a regular basis, for the cooling system to work effectively. Inspect the radiator thoroughly, and ask the vendor when it was last cleaned. Re-cored radiators are available.

Clutch

The clutch should be light and smooth in operation. Some cheap-end aftermarket clutch kits use cover plates with inappropriate springing, leading to a heavy pedal. If the clutch feels heavy, this could be the issue. Clutch judder can be caused by either oil contamination or soft gearbox mounts – or both – and should not be present.

Engine modifications

Imps tend to see their fair share of engine modification work, from twin carburettors to 998cc wet-liner conversions. Assess the quality of the work that has been carried out, and look at any paperwork that supports the modification work. Bear in mind that some performance camshafts may produce significantly more power than standard, but can be unpleasant to drive around town. If you are in any doubt, it is worth getting a second opinion from an Imp expert as to what as been done.

Brakes

Imp brakes are a very simple single circuit drum system – on Imp Sports and Stilettos there was a factory-fitted servo to boost braking effort. This servo was fitted in the front of early Sports, and then in the rear on the passenger side inner wing on cars, thereafter. Check the condition of the fluid – if it looks very dark, it could be an indicator that it hasn't been changed for a long time. Cylinders can seize, leading to brake imbalance and a lack of braking effort. The servo has an unkind habit of failing, leading to the brake fluid being sucked into the induction system of the engine, where it is burnt. A great many cars have had the servos removed for this reason.

Many cars will have had a disc brake conversion fitted; there are three main types, based on Vauxhall Viva, Nissan Micra or Ford Fiesta components. As brakes are key to safety, make sure that any such conversion has been done to a high standard – home-made conversions should be viewed with caution, but the kits sold by some specialists tend to be of a good quality.

Suspension ④ ③ ② ①

Imps feature independent suspension all round, with coil springs and telescopic dampers. Original springs can sag at the back, causing a nose-up stance; however, many Imps will have now been fitted with lowered 'Monte Carlo' springs. Check that any modifications to the suspension have been done properly – cut down springs, for example, rarely work well. Check the dampers for leaks, and 'bounce' each corner to see if the dampers are actually doing their job properly.

Lowered suspension can improve cornering at the expense of comfort.

An Imp should feel like a big go-kart on the road, so if the handling feels imprecise, it is likely that something is wrong. Bear in mind that tyre pressures can also make a massive difference, so investigate this, too, if the car does not drive well.

Wheels ④ ③ ② ①

All Imps left the factory with 12in diameter steel wheels. The very early cars had a 4J narrow rim and the Vans had a special, heavy-duty steel wheel. Some dealers offered alloy wheels as an extra for the Imp when they were new, but these would have been very expensive, and, again, would have been 12in diameter.

Many cars have been fitted with 13in alloy wheels to give more options for performance tyres – the options are far more limited in 12in.

Imps are unusual in that their wheels are located by the studs, not by the centre bore of the hub. Therefore, using wheels of the correct stud sizing is critical for safety. The cars should only ever have 4x4in pcd wheels – 100mm is close, but not right, and should never be used.

Many Imps have been tastefully modified – only you can decide if the modifications suit you.

Test drive (minimum 15 minutes)

In an ideal world, your test drive of a potential Imp purchase should last a minimum of 15 minutes and take in different road conditions, ideally with a stretch of fast-moving road, such as a motorway or dual carriageway.

The car should start readily, and be ready to move off from cold without too much hesitation. It should need some choke to begin with – but shouldn't need it for more than a couple of minutes, depending on the outside temperature.

The clutch biting point should be somewhere in the middle of the throw of the pedal – it is an idea to leave the handbrake up, and try setting off in third to test the clutch for slipping: if the engine stalls, the clutch is fine, but if it keeps revving, there is a problem.

You will find, if you have never driven an Imp before, that they require more revs than you may be used to. At low engine speeds, it is quite easy to stall the engine, and it may not pull cleanly. To get the most out of the engine, you do need to hang onto the gears a little more than most cars, and you may need to change down more often for hills than you are used to. However, this is normal – it's an engine built to rev.

Conversely, if the engine will not rev cleanly or pull hard in each gear, that could be something that needs investigating. Imps should thrive on revs, and if it seems to run out of puff in a particular gear, then something may be wrong.

The brakes should be sharp, precise, and should pull up in a straight line. However, if you have been used to driving a modern car with servo-assisted brakes, you may find that you need to use more effort than you are used to on a normal Imp. On Imp Sports and Stilettos, where the servo is fitted, this is lessened – listen for a clonk from the servo when operating, or if there is a lag between pressing the pedal and the brakes doing something, as this can be a sign of a sticking servo piston. Even an Imp on drum brakes should pull up quickly – find a deserted piece of road and try an emergency stop. It should pull up straight and true, and you should feel that you could lock the brakes – although there should be some control. Investigate snatching, or if the car veers to one side, on braking.

The ride should be very comfortable and sure-footed – Imps have quite a lot of suspension compliance as standard, and so, if it is banging and crashing over bumps, it may be an indicator that either the bushes are worn, or something else is wrong. If the car you are driving has lowered, uprated suspension, then, depending on what has been fitted, this can have a negative effect on the ride quality. The trade-off should be that the car should feel even more 'planted' on the road; if not, then it could be that the damping is set too hard – again, this depends on what has been fitted, and could be adjustable.

On your test drive, watch the temperature gauge, if fitted. It should rise up to just over half, and then drop down a touch when the thermostat opens – if it doesn't, ask the vendor what thermostat has been fitted, and be cautious of cars without thermostats fitted, as this can be to hide underlying faults.

On fast roads, even a standard Imp should have no trouble in holding 60mph, although you may be surprised by the engine speed to maintain that. Keep an eye on the temperature gauge – it may creep up a little on hills, but should drop again going down the other side. If it creeps and keeps creeping, there could be a fault with the cooling system.

The heater should produce some heat during a 15 minute drive – be cautious of any car where the owner says the heater never gets hot, as that is an indication that there is a fault with either the pipework, the heater matrix or the heater control valve. If there is no sign of overheating and yet there is no heat from the heater, one possible reason could be that the heater control valve has stuck. However, if the engine does get a little hot, then re-examine the engine carefully, and quiz the owner.

Engine and transmission noise should be well damped from the passenger compartment – the engine may boom at some speeds, depending on the exhaust system fitted, but, with either a standard or Imp Sport exhaust, the engine should never be intrusive. The transmission should be near-silent – any whine, whirring or grinding is an indicator that the transaxle is past its best.

The steering should be light and very responsive. Some cars are fitted with very small steering wheels and wide front tyres, which can make them grip the road well at the expense of the delicacy of the steering input. There should not be excessive vibration through the steering wheel – this is common on cars with worn steering components, as there isn't much weight on the front to damp this out. You should be able to feel the road through the wheel, but any vibrations need investigating.

Assess the driver's seat after 15 minutes of driving – some sagging seats will become fairly uncomfortable fairly quickly, and this could be an indicator that the seats fitted to your potential purchase are in need of some work.

Evaluation procedure

Add up the points scored!
144 to 152 points = excellent, possibly concours
108 to 143 points = good to very good
73 to 107 points = average
36 to 72 points = poor

Cars scoring over 101 should be completely usable, requiring only routine maintenance and car to be kept in good condition. Cars scoring below 73 will probably require a full restoration. Those scoring between 74 and 100 will need a very careful assessment of the work necessary, and its cost, in order to reach a realistic valuation.

10 Auctions
– sold! Another way to buy your dream

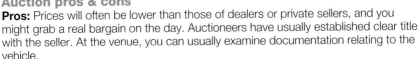

Auction pros & cons
Pros: Prices will often be lower than those of dealers or private sellers, and you might grab a real bargain on the day. Auctioneers have usually established clear title with the seller. At the venue, you can usually examine documentation relating to the vehicle.
Cons: You have to rely on a sketchy catalogue description of condition and history. The opportunity to inspect is limited, and you cannot drive the car. Auction cars are often a little below par and may require some work. It's easy to overbid. There will usually be a buyer's premium to pay in addition to the auction hammer price.

Which auction?
Auctions by established auctioneers are advertised in car magazines and on the auction houses' websites. A catalogue, or a simple printed list of the lots for auctions might only be available a day or two ahead, though often lots are listed and pictured on auctioneers' websites much earlier. Contact the auction company to ask if previous auction selling prices are available, as this is useful information (details of past sales are often available on websites).

Catalogue, entry fee and payment details
When you purchase the catalogue of the vehicles in the auction, it often acts as a ticket allowing two people to attend the viewing days and the auction. Catalogue details tend to be comparatively brief, but will include information such as 'one owner from new, low mileage, full service history,' etc. It will usually show a guide price to give you some idea of what to expect to pay, and will tell you what is charged as a 'Buyer's premium.' The catalogue will also contain details of acceptable forms of payment. At the fall of the hammer, an immediate deposit is usually required, the balance payable within 24 hours. If the plan is to pay by cash, there may be a cash limit. Some auctions will accept payment by debit card. Sometimes credit or charge cards are acceptable, but will often incur an extra charge. A bank draft or bank transfer will have to be arranged in advance with your own bank, as well as with the auction house. No car will be released before *all* payments are cleared. If delays occur in payment transfers, then storage costs can accrue.

Buyer's premium
A buyer's premium will be added to the hammer price: *don't* forget this in your calculations. It is not usual for there to be a further state tax or local tax on the purchase price and/or on the buyer's premium.

Viewing
In some instances it's possible to view on the day, or days before, as well as in the hours prior to, the auction. There are auction officials available who are willing to help out by opening engine and luggage compartments and to allow you to inspect the interior. While the officials may start the engine for you, a test drive is out of the question. Crawling under and around the car as much as you want is permitted, but

you can't suggest that the car you are interested in be jacked up, or attempt to do the job yourself. You can also ask to see any documentation available.

Bidding

Before you take part in the auction, *decide your maximum bid – and stick to it!*

It may take a while for the auctioneer to reach the lot you are interested in, so use that time to observe how other bidders behave. When it's the turn of your car, attract the auctioneer's attention and make an early bid. The auctioneer will then look to you for a reaction every time another bid is made, usually the bids will be in fixed increments until the bidding slows, when smaller increments will often be accepted before the hammer falls. If you want to withdraw from the bidding, make sure the auctioneer understands your intentions – a vigorous shake of the head when he or she looks to you for the next bid should do the trick!

Assuming that you are the successful bidder, the auctioneer will note your card or paddle number, and, from that moment on, you will be responsible for the vehicle.

If the car is unsold, either because it failed to reach the reserve, or because there was little interest, it may be possible to negotiate with the owner, via the auctioneers, after the sale is over.

Successful bid

There are two more items to think about. How to get the car home, and insurance. If you can't drive the car, your own or a hired trailer is one way; another is to have the vehicle shipped using the facilities of a local company. The auction house will also have details of companies specialising in the transfer of cars.

Insurance for immediate cover can usually be purchased on site, but it may be more cost-effective to make arrangements with your own insurance company in advance, and then call to confirm the full details.

eBay & other online auctions?

eBay & other online auctions could land you a car at a bargain price, though you'd be foolhardy to bid without examining the car first, something most vendors encourage. A useful feature of eBay is that the geographical location of the car is shown, so you can narrow your choices to those within a realistic radius of home. Be prepared to be outbid in the last few moments of the auction. Remember, your bid is binding and that it will be very, very difficult to get restitution in the case of a crooked vendor fleecing you – *caveat emptor!*

Be aware that some cars offered for sale in online auctions are 'ghost' cars. *Don't* part with *any* cash without being sure that the vehicle does actually exist and is as described (usually pre-bidding inspection is possible).

Auctioneers

Barrett-Jackson www.barrett-jackson.com/ Bonhams www.bonhams.com/ British Car Auctions (BCA) www.bca-europe.com or www.british-car-auctions. co.uk/ Cheffins www.cheffins.co.uk/ Christies www.christies.com/ Coys www. coys.co.uk/ EBay www.ebay.com or www.ebay.co.uk/ H&H www.classic-auctions.co.uk/ RM www.rmauctions.com/ Shannons www.shannons.com.au/ Silver www.silverauctions.com.

11 Paperwork
– correct documentation is essential!

The paper trail
Classic, collector and prestige cars usually come with a large portfolio of paperwork, accumulated and passed on by a succession of proud owners. This documentation represents the real history of the car, and from it can be deduced the level of care the car has received, how much it's been used, which specialists have worked on it, and the dates of major repairs and restorations. All of this information will be priceless to you as the new owner, so be very wary of cars with little paperwork to support their claimed history.

Registration documents
All countries/states have some form of registration for private vehicles, whether its like the American 'pink slip' system or the British 'log book' system.

It is essential to check that the registration document is genuine, that it relates to the car in question, and that all the vehicle's details are correctly recorded, including chassis/VIN and engine numbers (if these are shown). If you are buying from the previous owner, his or her name and address will be recorded in the document: this will not be the case if you are buying from a dealer.

In the UK, the current (Euro-aligned) registration document is named 'V5C,' and is printed in coloured sections of blue, green and pink. The blue section relates to the car specification, the green section has details of the new owner, and the pink section is sent to the DVLA, in the UK, when the car is sold. A small section in yellow deals with selling the car within the motor trade.

In the UK, the DVLA will provide details of earlier keepers of the vehicle, upon payment of a small fee, and much can be learned in this way.

If the car has a foreign registration, there may be expensive and time-consuming formalities to complete. Do you really want the hassle?

Roadworthiness certificate
Most country/state administrations require that vehicles are regularly tested to prove that they are safe to use on the public highway and do not produce excessive emissions. In the UK, that test (the 'MoT') is carried out at approved testing stations, for a fee. In the USA, the requirement varies, but most states insist on an emissions test every two years as a minimum, while the police are charged with pulling over unsafe-looking vehicles.

In the UK, the test is required on an annual basis once a vehicle becomes three years old. Of particular relevance for older cars is that the certificate issued includes the mileage reading recorded at the test date and, therefore, becomes an independent record of that car's history. Ask the seller if previous certificates are available. Without an MoT, the vehicle should be trailered to its new home, unless you insist that a valid MoT is part of the deal. (Not such a bad idea, this, as at least you will know the car was roadworthy on the day it was tested – and you don't need to wait for the old certificate to expire before having the test done.)

Road licence
The administration of every country/state charges some kind of tax for the use of its

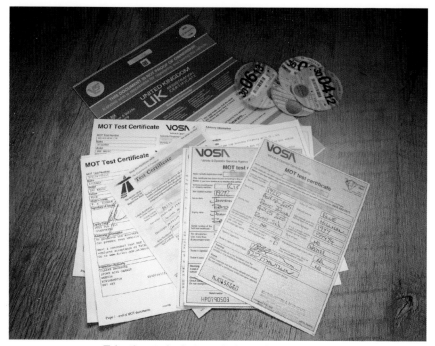

Take time to look through the car's paperwork.

road system, the actual form of the 'road licence' and, how it is displayed, varying enormously country to country and state to state.

Changed legislation in the UK means that the seller of a car must surrender any existing road fund licence, and it is the responsibility of the new owner to re-tax the vehicle at the time of purchase and before the car can be driven on the road. It's therefore vital to see the Vehicle Registration Certificate (V5C) at the time of purchase, and to have access to the New Keeper Supplement (V5C/2), allowing the buyer to obtain road tax immediately.

If the car is untaxed because it has not been used for a period of time, the owner has to inform the licensing authorities, otherwise the vehicle's date-related registration number will be lost and there will be a painful amount of paperwork to get it re-registered.

Whatever the form of the 'road licence,' it must relate to the vehicle carrying it and must be present and valid if the car is to be driven on the public highway legally. The value of the license will depend on the length of time it will continue to be valid.

In the UK, if a car is untaxed because it has not been used for a period of time, the owner has to inform the licensing authorities, otherwise the vehicle's date-related registration number will be lost and there will be a painful amount of paperwork to get it re-registered. Also, in the UK, vehicles more than 40 years old qualify for free road fund licence – you must still apply in the normal way, but the cost is zero. Car clubs can often provide formal proof that a particular car qualifies for this valuable concession.

Certificates of authenticity

For many makes of collectible car, it is possible to get a certificate proving the age and authenticity (eg engine and chassis numbers, paint colour and trim) of a particular vehicle, these are sometimes called 'Heritage Certificates' and, if the car comes with one of these, it is a definite bonus. If you want to obtain one, the relevant owners' club is the best starting point.

If the car has been used in European classic car rallies, it may have a FIVA (Federation Internationale des Vehicules Anciens) certificate. The so-called 'FIVA Passport,' or 'FIVA Vehicle Identity Card,' enables organisers and participants to recognise whether or not a particular vehicle is suitable for individual events. If you want to obtain such a certificate go to <www.fbhvc.co.uk> or <www.fiva.org>; there will be similar organisations in other countries, too.

Valuation certificate

Hopefully, the vendor will have a recent valuation certificate, or letter signed by a recognised expert stating how much he, or she, believes the particular car to be worth (such documents, together with photos, are usually needed to get 'agreed value' insurance). Generally such documents should act only as confirmation of your own assessment of the car, rather than a guarantee of value, as the expert has probably not seen the car in the flesh. The easiest way to find out how to obtain a formal valuation is to contact the owners' club.

Service history

Often these cars will have been serviced at home by enthusiastic (and hopefully capable) owners for a good number of years. Nevertheless, try to obtain as much service history and other paperwork pertaining to the car as you can. Naturally, dealer stamps, or specialist garage receipts score most points in the value stakes. However, anything helps in the great authenticity game, items like the original bill of sale, handbook, parts invoices and repair bills, adding to the story and the character of the car. Even a brochure correct to the year of the car's manufacture is a useful document, and something that you could well have to search hard to locate in future years. If the seller claims that the car has been restored, then expect receipts and other evidence from a specialist restorer.

If the seller claims to have carried out regular servicing, ask what work was completed, when, and seek some evidence of it being carried out. Your assessment of the car's overall condition should tell you whether the seller's claims are genuine.

Restoration photographs

If the seller tells you that the car has been restored, then expect to be shown a series of photographs taken while the restoration was under way. Pictures taken at various stages, and from various angles, should help you gauge the thoroughness of the work. If you buy the car, ask if you can have all the photographs, as they form an important part of the vehicle's history. It's surprising how many sellers are happy to part with their car and accept your cash, but want to hang on to their photographs! In the latter event, you may be able to persuade the vendor to get a set of copies made.

12 What's it worth?
– let your head rule your heart

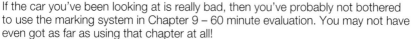

Condition

If the car you've been looking at is really bad, then you've probably not bothered to use the marking system in Chapter 9 – 60 minute evaluation. You may not have even got as far as using that chapter at all!

If you did use the marking system in Chapter 9, you'll know whether the car is in Excellent (maybe Concours), Good, Average or Poor condition or, perhaps, somewhere in-between these categories.

Many classic/collector car magazines run a regular price guide. If you haven't bought the latest editions, do so now, and compare their suggested values for the model you are thinking of buying: also look at the auction prices they're reporting. Values have been fairly stable for some time, but some models will always be more sought-after than others. Trends can change too. The values published in the magazines tend to vary from one magazine to another, as do their scales of condition, so read carefully the guidance notes they provide. Bear in mind that a car that is truly a recent show winner could be worth more than the highest scale published. Assuming that the car you have in mind is not in show/concours condition, then relate the level of condition that you judge the car to be in with the appropriate guide price. How does the figure compare with the asking price? Before you begin haggling with the seller, consider what affect any variation from standard specification might have on the car's value.

If you are buying from a dealer, remember there will be a dealer's premium on the price.

Desirable options/extras

Singer and Sunbeam models always command a higher price than Hillman-badged cars. Singer Chamois models have very nice interiors, the early cars having real wood trim on the dashboard and door cappings. From the factory, these cars had better soundproofing and better seats, giving the cars a genuine sense of luxury.

Of the Singer range, the Rootes-built Chamois Sport models are amongst the most desirable – and probably the hardest to find. There are plenty of Singers that have been uprated to sport specification, but very few are genuine cars.

The Sunbeam models again command massive interest due to their performance, and many standard cars will have had modification work to give similar specifications. Again, Sunbeams are hard to find – with Rootes cars the most tricky to locate, and the four-headlamp 1970s cars the ones that people seem to want the most.

Coupé models are always in demand, as arguably they are very pretty cars. The Sunbeam Stiletto and the Rootes-era Singer Chamois coupé are probably the most highly sought after, and have the highest prices as a result. The later four-headlamp Singer Chamois coupé is very hard to find, but the interior isn't quite as nice as the early car. Hillman Imp Californians are probably just as rare, and command a price premium over an equivalent saloon.

Huskies and vans have their own legion of fans, but, due to their rarity (utility vehicles rarely survive in quantity), will cost significantly more than a saloon.

Sunbeam Stilettos command a price premium over other variants.

There was a late-model, limited edition called the Caledonian – this had cherry red paint, a tartan interior, a pushbutton radio, and a heated rear screen.

Undesirable features
As a rule of thumb, the post Chrysler Mk3 Imps – especially the standard Hillman-badged ones – are less desirable than the earlier Rootes-built cars. There are many reasons for this, but that isn't to say that the late cars aren't great – they are often better to drive in standard form than the early ones.

Early Mk1 cars had a more fragile engine (curly edge block), more fragile cooling system and clutch. Depending on your point of view, the early car's pneumatic throttle and autochoke can be desirable or undesirable.

Striking a deal
Negotiate on the basis of your condition assessment, mileage, and fault rectification cost. Also take into account the car's specification. Be realistic about the value, but don't be completely intractable: a small compromise on the part of the vendor or buyer will often facilitate a deal at little real cost.

www.velocebooks.com / www.veloce.co.uk
Details of all current books • New book news • Special offers • Gift vouchers • Forum

49

13 Do you really want to restore?
– it'll take longer and cost more than you think

Let's get one thing out of the way immediately: buying a restoration project and restoring it, even by yourself, is likely to cost far more than buying a good car in the first place. Professional restorations will run into thousands of pounds, because the hours spent on labour alone will outstrip the price of a good car.

However, there are a few good reasons for choosing a restoration project. Firstly, there is the emotive reason – finding a sad, forgotten classic car in a barn is a romantic dream for many of us. The reality is often very different, but the emotional connection to a inanimate object cannot be ignored.

It is also fair to say that due to the rarity of some variants of the Imp, finding a perfect example of the exact model you are looking for may be tricky, and you may find that the only option is to buy a car needing work.

Restoring a car takes the gamble out of buying a classic car, to a degree. Sometimes it is hard to be sure what is under shiny paintwork – have previous repairs been done correctly, or is it a mass of wire-mesh and filler? If you restore the car yourself, or have the work done by a trusted restorer, then you remove this concern.

The fact remains that finding 'restoration projects' is usually easier than finding good cars for sale – most enthusiasts tend to hold onto good examples now, and so cars needing work are far more common. The trick is working out whether you are looking at a restoration project, a spares car, or a basket case – there is a difference: avoid basket case cars.

A restoration project car should be complete, it also should be 'restorable' in that it shouldn't be too rotten, or missing too many parts. Often cars that are offered for sale as 'restoration projects' are in very poor condition. Replacing sills, wheelarches and even small sections of the floor should not be underestimated in terms of time and money expenditure, but couple that with locating missing or worn out rare trim, badges or even mechanical components can be the death of a project.

Whenever you consider a project car, whatever rust you can see is usually the tip of the iceberg. For example: it costs the same to replace a wheelarch that has

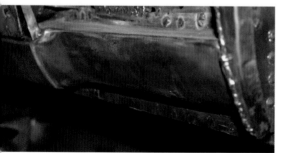

Sill repairs to this standard are costly and time-consuming.

one bubble or a great mass of holes. It gets more expensive if someone has tried 'repairing' it in the past and you need to unpick what a previous owner has done. Therefore it is often best to buy poorer condition original cars than superficially better 'repaired' ones.

Whatever you do, never buy a restoration project car unseen via eBay, just based on a description and some pictures … it's unlikely to end well.

14 Paint problems

– bad complexion, including dimples, pimples and bubbles

Paint faults generally occur due lack of protection/maintenance, or to poor preparation prior to a respray or touch-up. Some of the following conditions may be present in the car you're looking at:

Orange peel
This appears as an uneven paint surface, similar to the appearance of the skin of an orange. The fault is caused by the failure of atomised paint droplets to flow into each other when they hit the surface. It's sometimes possible to rub out the effect with proprietary paint cutting/rubbing compound, or very fine grades of abrasive paper. A respray may be necessary, in severe cases. Consult a bodywork repairer/paint shop for advice on the particular car.

Cracking
Severe cases are likely to have been caused by too heavy an application of paint (or filler beneath the paint). Also, insufficient stirring of the paint before application can lead to the components being improperly mixed, and cracking can result. Incompatibility with the paint already on the panel can have a similar effect. To rectify the problem, it is necessary to rub down to a smooth, sound finish, before respraying the problem area.

Crazing
Sometimes the paint takes on a crazed, rather than a cracked, appearance

Crazing and cracking can only be resolved by bare-metal repainting.

when the problems mentioned under 'Cracking' are present. This problem can also be caused by a reaction between the underlying surface and the paint. Paint removal and respraying the problem area is usually the only solution.

Blistering
Almost always caused by corrosion of the metal beneath the paint. Usually perforation will be found in the metal, and the damage will usually be worse than that suggested by the area of blistering. The metal will have to be repaired before repainting.

Micro blistering
Usually the result of an economy respray where inadequate heating has allowed moisture to settle on the car before spraying. Consult a paint specialist, but, in most cases, damaged paint will have to be removed before partial or full respraying. Can also be caused by car covers that don't 'breathe.'

Faded paint – this car was originally royal blue!

Fading

Some colours, especially reds, are prone to fading, if subjected to strong sunlight for long periods without the benefit of polish protection. Sometimes proprietary paint restorers and/or paint cutting/rubbing compounds will retrieve the situation. Often a respray is the only real solution.

Peeling

Often a problem with metallic paintwork when the sealing lacquer becomes damaged and begins to peel off. Poorly applied paint may also peel. The remedy is to strip and begin again!

Dimples

Dimples in the paintwork are caused by the residue of polish (particularly silicone types) not being removed properly before respraying. Paint removal and repainting is the only solution.

Dents

Small dents are usually easily cured by the 'Dentmaster,' or equivalent process, that sucks or pushes out the dent (as long as the paint surface is still intact). Companies offering dent removal services usually come to your home: consult your telephone directory.

www.velocebooks.com / www.veloce.co.uk
Details of all current books • New book news • Special offers • Gift vouchers • Forum

52

15 Problems due to lack of use

– just like their owners, Hillman Imps need exercise!

Cars, like humans, are at their most efficient if they exercise regularly. A run of at least ten miles, once a week, is recommended for classics.

Seized components
- Slave and master cylinders can seize
- The clutch may seize if the plate becomes stuck to the flywheel because of corrosion
- Handbrakes (parking brakes) can seize if the cables and linkages rust
- Pistons can seize in the bores due to corrosion

Fluids
- Old, acidic oil can corrode bearings
- Uninhibited coolant can corrode internal waterways and even the top face of the head. In extreme cases, this can render the head beyond repair. Lack of antifreeze can cause cracks in the block or head. Silt settling and solidifying can cause overheating – it sets hard behind cylinder number four
- Brake fluid absorbs water from the atmosphere, and should be renewed every two years. Old fluid with a high water content can cause corrosion and pistons to seize (freeze), and can cause brake failure when the water turns to vapour near hot braking components

Tyre problems
- Tyres that have had the weight of the car on them in a single position for some time will develop flat spots, resulting in some (usually temporary) vibration. The tyre walls may have cracks or (blister-type) bulges, meaning new tyres are needed. Tyres do have date codes – it is worth looking up their age. Old tyres can fail without warning

Flat tyres may have weakened side walls.

Shock absorbers (dampers)
• With lack of use, the dampers will lose their elasticity, or even seize. Creaking, groaning and stiff suspension are signs of this problem

Rubber and plastic
• Radiator hoses may have perished and split, possibly resulting in the loss of all coolant. Window and door seals can harden and leak. Gaiters/boots can crack. Wiper blades will harden

Electrics
• The battery will be of little use if it has not been charged for many months

• Earthing/grounding problems are common when the connections have corroded. Old bullet-type and spade-type electrical connectors commonly rust/corrode and will need disconnecting, cleaning and protection (eg Vaseline)
• Sparkplug electrodes will often have corroded, in an unused engine
• Wiring insulation can harden and fail

Rotting exhaust system
• Exhaust gas contains a high water content, so exhaust systems corrode very quickly from the inside, when the car is not used

Charging systems often suffer on cars that are used infrequently.

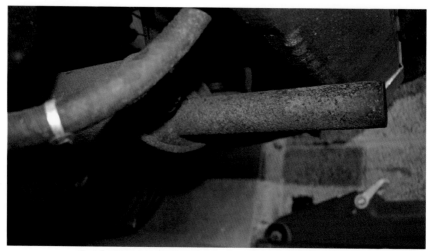

Condensation corrodes exhaust systems from the inside.

16 The Community
– key people, organisations & companies in the Hillman Imp world

As the Imp has historically been a car that has been maintained and serviced by its owners, there aren't many specialists who are geared up for this task. However, most classic car-friendly garages can provide this service, should it be needed.

Specialists

Supplier of new, used and remanufactured parts
Malcolm Anderson Imp Parts
Bay House, Main Road
Norton Fitzwarren
Nr Taunton
Somerset TA2 6QS
Tel: 01823 350360
www.malcolmanderson.co.uk

Engine parts, including competition parts
Corley Conversions (Ben Boult)
Tel: 01926 612432
www.corley-conversions.co.uk

Engine parts, machining and reconditioning
Maynard Engines Ltd
Unit 10, Merrets Mill
Woodchester
Gloucestershire GL5 5EX
Tel: 01453 833185

Service, repairs, MoT, and new and used parts
Merlin Motors
Chapel Street
Caerwys
Mold
Flintshire
Tel: 01352 720280

Supplier of new parts and spares
Speedy Spares Ltd (incorporating RJ Grimes (Coulsdon) Ltd)
19-25 Old Shoreham Road
Portslade
East Sussex BN41 1SP
Tel: 01273 417889
www.speedyspares.co.uk

Owners' club
The Imp Club
Established in 1980, the Imp Club is dedicated to keeping the Imp alive. With members throughout the UK and the rest of world, the club has a vibrant website and forum, plus local area centre meetings held all over the country. The club has links to Imp motorsport activity, and has a spares service, too. The club organises events all over the UK, and into mainland Europe, its main event being the National Weekend held in August. www.theimpclub.co.uk

Useful books
Rootes Group produced its own Workshop Manual for the Imp, which can still be found secondhand.

Grainger, Rod, *Hillman Imp Owner's Workshop Manual,* Haynes
ISBN 0 900550 22 8

Griffiths, Willy, *Tuning Imps,*
Bookmarque Publishing
ISBN 1 870519 42 6

Millington, Tim *Hillman Imps Tuning – Overhaul – Servicing,*
Minster Lovell ISBN 1 870519 05 1

Henshaw, Peter & David, *Apex, The Inside Story of the Hillman Imp,*
Bookmarque Publishing
ISBN 1 870519 11 6

Coulter, Paul, *Our Hillman Imp,*
Argyll Publishing
ISBN 0 900550 22 8

17 Vital statistics
– essential data at your fingertips

Imp Range:	1963 to 1976
Engine Size:	875cc
Power:	(STD) 39bhp @ 5000rpm
	(Sport) 51bhp @ 6100rpm
Number produced:	440,032

Summary of models produced
Mk1 Hillman Imp
1963-1965
High waist trim, thin front seats, thin wheel rims, positive earth, metal-ended dashboard with binnacle for speedo, star-wheel door latches, high pivot front suspension, early cars had automatic choke and pneumatic throttle.

Early Mk1 Hillman Imp.

Mk2 Hillman Imp
1965-1968
Revised interior with thicker seats, revised padded ends to dashboard with binnacle for speedo. Deluxe and basic had high waist trim as before, Super Imp had interior door cappings and wide trim fitted lower down the wings. A few early cars had high pivot front suspension, but changed to low pivot for majority. Wider 5J rims. Later cars gained square-edged (stronger) engine block and a bigger valve cylinder head. A few badging changes, but otherwise as Mk1.

Hillman Super Imp Mk2.

Mk3 (facelift) Hillman Imp
1968-1976
Totally new brightwork and badges for Basic, Deluxe and Super models. Round dial dashboard introduced. Welded, rather than stitched seats. Deluxe and Basic had no glovebox – Supers had better door cards, door cappings and high quality carpets. Anti-burst door locks were fitted to all models. From around 1974, uprated cylinder head fitted with Sport camshaft (de-tuned with small choke carburettor), gradual introduction of heated rear screen, alternator and fuse box.

Hillman Imp Super Mk3.

Singer Chamois Mk3 (left) and Singer Chamois Mk1 (right).

Singer Chamois Mk1/Mk2
1964-1968
Bodyshell as Hillman, but with revised grille, side chrome trims and colour flash down the side. Wood dashboard and door cappings, with improved seats and carpets. 4.5J rims.

1966 Singer Chamois Mk2.

Singer Chamois Sport Mk2
1966-1968
As Singer Chamois above, but with twin carburettor Imp Sport engine, slatted engine cover for extra cooling, reclining seats and servo assisted brakes.

Singer Chamois Mk3 (facelift)
1968-1970
As per Mk3 Imp Super, but with four headlamp front panel and reclining front seats (optional). Wide side trims infilled in light grey rather than black. Different badging. Imitation wood dashboard and door cappings. Oil pressure gauge fitted.

Sunbeam Imp Sport
1966-1968
As per Singer Chamois Sport, but with different front badging, wide side trim as per Super Imp, no side colour flash, dashboard and door caps wrapped in black vinyl rather than polished wood. Sunburst wheel trims. Twin carburettor Sport engine, servo assisted brakes.

Sunbeam Sport
1968-1970
As per Imp Super, with two headlamp front panel, wide alloy badge with 'Sunbeam' insert, slatted engine cover, reclining seats, twin carburettor Imp Sport engine, servo assisted brakes. Sunburst wheel trims.

Sunbeam Imp Sport
1970-1976
Bodyshell as per Singer Chamois Mk3, with four headlamp front. Different badges. Slatted engine cover, reclining

Sunbeam Imp Sport Mk3.

seats, imitation wood dashboard and door caps, twin carburettor Imp Sport engine, servo assisted brakes, Sunburst wheel trims.

Coupés
Hillman Imp Californian
1966-1968
Trim and brightwork as per Imp Super. Unique badges and front grille. Reclining front seats, split folding rear seats.

Hillman Imp Californian 1967.

Hillman Imp Californian (Mk3)
1968-1970
Trim and brightwork as per Imp Super. Full width alloy front panel. Reclining front seats, split folding rear seats.

Singer Chamois coupé
1967-1968
Trim and engine as per Singer Chamois. Reclining front seats, split folding rear seats.

Singer Chamois (Mk3)
1968-1970
Trim and engine as per Singer Chamois, with four headlamp front panel. Reclining front seats, split folding rear seats.

Sunbeam Stiletto
1967-1968
Mechanicals as per Sunbeam Imp Sport. Unique dashboard with round dials, unique three-spoke steering wheel, reclining front seats and split rear seats trimmed in perforated 'Amblair' vinyl. Vinyl roof and four headlamp front panel, full length alloy trim along top of sill. Sunburst wheel trims.

Sunbeam Stiletto 1970.

Sunbeam Stiletto
1968-1972
As per the earlier model, but fitted with anti-burst door locks, seats as per Imp Californian, but trimmed in Amblair. Alloy trim along top of sill deleted.

Van/Husky
Commer Imp van
1966-1968
Van bodyshell, star-wheel door locks, thin back red front seat (passenger seat optional), wings badge on front panel, binnacle dashboard, low compression engine, heavy-duty rims, rubber floor covering. Heavy-duty suspension and driveshafts.

Commer Imp van.

Hillman Imp van.

Hillman Imp van
1968-1970
As above, but with anti-burst door locks, 'lozenge' badge on front panel, Mk3 Imp Basic seats in black.

Hillman Husky 1970.

Hillman Husky
1967-1968
Bodyshell as Imp van, but with rear side windows (with sliding section), unique rear seat assembly, brightwork unique to Husky, trim and mechanicals as per equivalent age Imp deluxe but with heavy-duty suspension as per van.

Hillman Husky
1968-1970
As above, but with full width alloy front panel badge, simplified brightwork, anti-burst door locks.

Rare/limited edition models

There was a Rallye version offered in the mid 1960s, with a 998cc wet-liner engine – this was offered for all saloon models. These are incredibly rare, as most were converted into competition cars, so it is highly unlikely that you will be offered one of these.

The 'Spring Special' was offered in 1967, based on the Imp Super or Singer Chamois – these had metallic pewter-grey or metallic gold paint, US-specification bumpers with larger over-riders and a Canadian specification heater (larger). Again, these are rare, and, aside from the differences mentioned above, they are, to all intents and purposes, identical to their 'base' models.

There was a run out model called the 'Caledonian' made in 1976. These were based on Imp Deluxes, and were painted Cherry red with white side stripes. They featured a tartan interior, a push button radio, a heated rear screen and sunburst wheeltrims.

The Essential Buyer's Guide™ series ...

Also from Veloce Publishing –

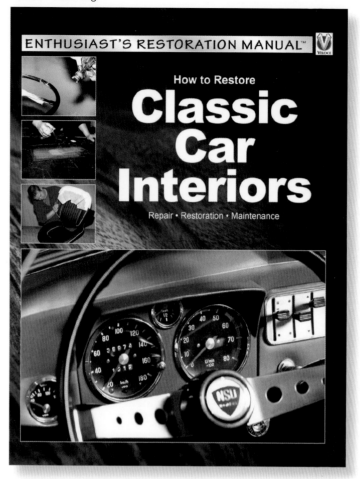

ENTHUSIAST'S RESTORATION MANUAL™

How to Restore
Classic Car Interiors
Repair • Restoration • Maintenance

Packed with restoration know-how on all kinds of interior fittings in your classic
car: carpets, headlinings, seats, wood and synthetic material parts, instruments,
steering wheels: even how to succeed in making your radio sound just like new!
Includes reproduction of parts on a 3D printer.

ISBN: 978-1-845849-83-2
Paperback • 27x20.7cm • 144 pages • 608 pictures

For more info on Veloce titles, visit our website at www.veloce.co.uk
• email: info@veloce.co.uk • Tel: +44(0)1305 260068

ROOTES CARS
of the 1950s, 1960s & 1970s
Hillman, Humber, Singer, Sunbeam & Talbot

A Pictorial History
David Rowe

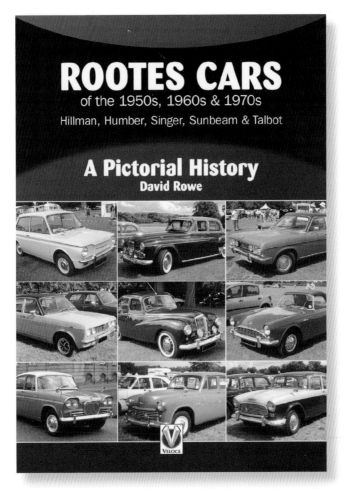

VELOCE

Rootes Cars of the '50s, '60s & '70s is the only full-colour comprehensive guide to all Hillman, Humber, Sunbeam, Singer & Talbot cars & vans, built from 1950 until the end of production in the 1970s. With model-by-model descriptions and detailed technical information, this is an invaluable Rootes resource.

ISBN: 978-1-845849-93-1
Paperback • 21x14.8cm • 168 pages • 1083 colour and b&w pictures

For more info on Veloce titles, visit our website at www.veloce.co.uk
• email: info@veloce.co.uk • Tel: +44(0)1305 260068

Index